for Sam —
Happy Birthday!
x

Mrs Scrooge

Mrs Scrooge

Carol Ann Duffy

with illustrations by Posy Simmonds

PICADOR

First published 2009 by Picador
an imprint of Pan Macmillan, a division of Macmillan Publishers Limited
Pan Macmillan, 20 New Wharf Road, London N1 9RR
Basingstoke and Oxford
Associated companies throughout the world
www.panmacmillan.com

ISBN 978-0-330-51511-5

3 5 7 9 8 6 4

A CIP catalogue record for this book is available
from the British Library.

Manufactured in Belgium by Proost

Visit *www.picador.com* to read more about all our books
and to buy them. You will also find features, author interviews and
news of any author events, and you can sign up for e-newsletters
so that you're always first to hear about our new releases.

Mrs Scrooge

Scrooge doornail-dead, his widow, Mrs Scrooge, lived by herself in London Town. It was that time of year, the clocks long back, when shops were window-dressed with unsold tinsel, trinkets, toys, trivial pursuits, with sequinned dresses and designer suits, with chocolates, glacé fruits and marzipan, with Barbie, Action Man, with bubblebath and aftershave and showergel; the words *Noel* and *Season's Greetings* brightly mute in neon lights. The city bells had only just chimed three, but it was dusk already. It had not been light all day.

Mrs Scrooge sat googling at her desk,

                                Catchit the cat

curled at her feet; snowflakes tumbling to the ground
below the window, where a robin perched,
pecking at seeds. *Most turkeys,*
bred for their meat, are kept in windowless barns,
with some containing over 20,000 birds. Turkeys
are removed from their crates and hung from shackles
by their legs in moving lines. A small fire crackled
in the grate. *Their heads are dragged under*
a water bath – electrically charged – before their necks
are cut. Mrs Scrooge pressed *Print.*

                                She planned

to visit Marley's Supermarket *(Biggest Bargain Birds!)* at four.

4

Outside, snowier yet, and cold! Piercing, searching, biting cold.
The cold gnawed noses just as dogs gnaw bones. It iced
the mobile phones pressed tight to ears.

                                      The coldest Christmas Eve
in years saw Mrs Scrooge at Marley's, handing leaflets out.
The shoppers staggered past, weighed down with bags
or pushing trolleys crammed with breasts, legs, crowns, eggs,
sausages, giant stalks of brussels sprouts, carrots,
spuds, bouquets of broccoli, mange tout, courgettes, petits
pois, foie gras; with salmon, Stilton, pork pies, mince pies,
Christmas Pudding, custard,
port, gin, sherry, whisky,
fizz and plonk,
                all done on credit cards.

Most shook their head at Mrs Scrooge,
irked by her cry *"Find out how turkeys really die!"*
or shoved her leaflet in the pockets of their coats, unread,
or laughed and called back, *"Spoilsport! Ho! Ho! Ho!"*
Three hours went by like this.

                           The snow

                                      began to ease

as she walked home.

She hated waste, consumerism, Mrs Scrooge, foraged
in the London parks for chestnuts, mushrooms, blackberries,
ate leftovers, recycled, mended, passed on, purchased secondhand,
turned the heating down and put on layers, walked everywhere,
drank tap-water, used public libraries, possessed a wind-up radio,
switched off lights, lit candles (darkness is cheap and Mrs Scrooge
liked it) and would not spend *one penny* on a plastic bag.
She passed off-licences with *6 for 5*, bookshops with *3 for 2*,
food stores with *Buy 1 get 1 free*.

                                    Above her head,
the Christmas lights
                        danced like a river toward a sea of dark.
The National Power Grid moaned, endangered, like a whale.

The Thames flowed on as Mrs Scrooge proceeded on her way towards her rooms.

Nobody lived in the building now
but her, and all the other flats were boarded up.
Whatever the developers had offered Mrs Scrooge to move
could never be enough. She liked it where it was,
lurking in the corner of a yard, as though the house
had run there young, playing hide-and-seek,
and had forgotten the way out. She remembered
her first Christmas there with Scrooge,
the single stripey sweet
he'd given her that year, and every year.

But Scrooge was dead, no doubt of that, so why,
her key turning the lock, did she see in the knocker
Scrooge's face? His face to the life, staring back at her
with living grey-green eyes and opening metal lips!
As Mrs Scrooge looked fixedly at this,
it turned into a knocker once again.

U p the echoing stairs
to slippers, simple supper, candles, cocoa, cat,
went Mrs Scrooge; not scared, but oddly comforted
at glimpsing Scrooge's knockered face.
But still, she double-locked the door, put on her dressing gown
and sat down by the fire to sip her soup.
                                    The fire
was very low indeed, not much on such a bitter night,
so soon enough she went to bed – night-cap, bed-socks,
Scrooge's old pyjamas, hot water-bottle, Catchit's purr . . .
and then her own soft snore.

She dreamed of Scrooge,
                              of Christmas past,
of Christmas present, Christmas yet to come; dreams
that seemed to trap her in a snowstorm bowl –
newly-married, ice-skating with Scrooge,
two necks in one long, bright red, woolly scarf;
or hanging baubles on the tree;
or being surprised by mistletoe, his kiss, the taste of him –
but then her world was shaken violently
and she was kneeling by a grave, hearing a funeral bell . . .

Midnight rang out from St Paul's. She gasped awake.
The twice-locked door was open wide
and all the room was filled with light
and smelled of tangerines and cinnamon and wine.
A cheerful Ghost was perched and grinning on her bed,
now like a child, now like a wise old man,
with silver hair and berried holly for a crown
(and yet its shimmering dress was trimmed with flowers).
"*Good grief!*" said Mrs Scrooge. "*Who the hell are you?*"
The Ghost squealed with delight and clapped its hands
(a hard thing for a ghost to do, thought Mrs Scrooge).
"*I am the Ghost of Christmas Past,*" it trilled.
"*Now, rise! And walk with me.*"

It took her by the hand
then flew her through the bedroom wall. They stood at once
upon an open country road, with fields on either side.
The city had entirely gone, the darkness too;
it was a sparkling winter's day, all blinged with frost.
"I know this place!" cried Mrs Scrooge. *"I grew up here!*
We're near the village of Heath Row!
My family kept an orchard close to here."
They walked along the road, Mrs Scrooge recalling
every gate, and post, and tree.

"*T*hat way's Harmondsworth,"
she told the Ghost excitedly. "*Famous for Richard Cox,*
you know, who cultivated Cox's Orange Pippin."
The merry Ghost conjured an apple from the air.
She crunched delightedly. "*That way's Longford village;*
that way's the farm at Perry Oaks; and that way's Sipson Green!"
They'd reached the village now, a green, a row of houses and an Inn;
two fields away a farm, beyond that farm another farm;
the landscape glittering as if it were in love with light.
A laughing local bunch of lads ran by.
Mrs Scrooge went red!
"*I snogged that tall one once!*" she said.

"*T*hey're shadows,"
said the Ghost. "*They have no consciousness of us.*"
High in the sky there came an aeroplane, rare enough
to make the boys stand pointing at the endless, generous air
and yell out "*Merry Christmas!*" to the plane.

"*This is the past,
it cannot come again,*" went on the Ghost, "*It is the gift
your soul gives to your heart.*"
Mrs Scrooge stopped in the road and turned. "*Why show
me this?*" she asked. "*Because,*" the Ghost replied,
"*Scrooge sends a message from the grave –
keep going! You shall overcome!*"
"*No Runway Three!*" cried Mrs Scrooge,
the breath her words made
like a ghost itself, swooning, vanishing.

But when she looked,
the face of Christmas Past bent down,
just like a lover stoops to steal a kiss,
and then her lips were soft, then salty,
tasting tears, her own, and then she woke,
at home, and old, and all alone.

Not quite alone,
for Catchit dozed and snuggled at her feet,
visions of robin redbreasts in his head.

London's moon,
the moon of Shakespeare, Dickens, Oscar, Virginia Woolf,
shone down on silent theatres, banks, hotels,
on palaces and dosshouses and parks,

on Mrs Scrooge,
who lay, wide-eyed and fretful, in the dark. She heard
a scrabbling noise inside the chimney-breast
and sat bolt upright in her bed –

"*Who's there?*" she said —
then, with a thump, a flash,
                    a figure in a crimson Santa suit
glowed in the grate, as if the fire had taken human shape
and combed itself a beard from its smoke.
"*I am the Ghost of Christmas Present,*"
boomed the Ghost. "*Now rise, and come with me!*"

Before she knew it, Mrs Scrooge sat in a sleigh,
being pulled by reindeers through the starry sky,
tying a ribbon round the earth;
the Ghost of Christmas Present talking as they flew, naming
the oceans, forests, mountain ranges far below,
until the Arctic Circle rose beneath them like a moon.
They landed,
              skidding on the ice,
in a percussion of sharp hooves and jingling bells.

Tears, like opals,
                fell, then froze,
on Mrs Scrooge's cheeks as she looked.
She stood upon a continent of ice
which sparkled between sea and sky,
                                endless and dazzling,
as though the world kept all its treasure there;
                                a scale
which balanced poetry and prayer.

But then she heard a crackling, rumbling groan
and saw huge icebergs calving from the floe

into the sea;
then, further out, a polar bear, floating,

stranded,
on a raft of ice.

"*The Polar Ice Cap melting,*" said the Ghost.
"*Can mankind save it?*"
"*Yes, we can!*" cried Mrs Scrooge. "*We must!*"
"*I bring encouragement from Scrooge's dust,*" replied the Ghost.
"*Never give up. Don't think one ordinary human life
can make no difference — for it can!*"

The reindeers steamed and snorted in the snow.
Mrs Scrooge stretched out her hand to one,
stroking the warm, rough texture of its hide,
which seemed to alter, soften, into Catchit's fur!
The North Pole vanished like a snuffed-out flame.
She woke again.

"*O*ld fool!"
said Mrs Scrooge to herself. "*These are just dreams.*"
She pulled her blankets up beneath her chin
and lay there, worrying about large things and small.
The wall flickered with strange shadows, shifting shapes —
a turkey, and then a bear, and then a hooded form
which pointed at her silently,
until it swelled and stood and spoke!
"*I am the Ghost of Christmas Yet to Come! Rise now,
and follow me!*"

It took her in its arms like a bride
and flew her through a winter wood
towards a clearing

and an open grave,
around which mourners stood,

then put her down.
"*My family!*" said Mrs Scrooge. "*There's Bob!
And that's his lovely wife!
There are my grandchildren! Peter! Martha! Tiny Tim!
Look! They're my dearest friends, the Fezziwigs! Their girls!
Why are we here? Who died?*"

The Spirit pointed downward to the grave.
Mrs Scrooge crept near and peeped into a wormy, loamy hole.
She saw a cardboard coffin, crayoned brightly with a name,
cartooned with flowers, faces, animals,
covered with poems, kisses, hearts.

She turned . . .

At once, she stood beside the Ghost
inside a huge and crowded room,
her friends and family piling in!
In came a fiddler with a music-book
who started up a jig.

                   (Mrs Scrooge,
who loved a whirl,
restrained herself from dancing with the Ghost.)

In came Mrs Fezziwig, one vast substantial smile,
bearing a tray of home-made, warm mince pies; saying
"She would have wanted it this way!" In came
the Fezziwig girls with babies chuckling in their arms. In came
tall nephews arm-in-arm with little aunts.

                                 In came old comrades
with whom she'd marched in protest
against every kind of harm.

                         In they all came,
aglow with life and possibility, old and young;
away they went, twenty couples all at once,
gay and straight, down the middle, up and round again,
the beaming fiddler trying to saw his instrument in half!

T here never was

            such a wake!

More dancing, then more music, someone sang,

several shed tears;

then mince pies, cake, mulled wine, cold beer,

more wine, more beer;

then Mrs Scrooge heard a cheer

and there was Tiny Tim, up on a chair!

There was a hush.

           "A toast!"

cried Tiny Tim. *"To my grandmother! The best woman*

who ever was! She taught us all

to value everything!

           To give ourselves!

To live as if each day

           was Christmas Day!"

Another cheer and Mrs Scrooge's name rang out
from everybody's lips.
                              She seemed to float
above them; all the bright, familiar faces
                                          looking up,
raised glasses in the air.
She heard Bob say, "*She really had a wonderful life!*"
The Ghost of Christmas Yet to Come
                              pulled back its hood.
She looked into its smiling, loving, grey-green eyes
and understood.

Clash, clang, hammer, ding, dong, bell!
Bell, dong, ding, hammer, clang, clash!
It was St Paul's again,
                    gargling its morning bells,
the room her own;
                    and dribbling Catchit
staring down at her from her chest!
Quickly, Mrs Scrooge showered and dressed.
She flung open the window and leaned out –
a clear, bright, jovial, cold and glorious day!

The doorbell rang.
                    Down she hurried,
opened wide the door,
                              and in they poured,
taking the stairs two at a time – Bob, Bob's wife,
the grandchildren, the Fezziwigs,
their girls, babies, partners,
                              all shouting
"*Merry Christmas! Merry Christmas! Merry Christmas!*"

W hat news they had!
                              The credit crunch
had forced the property developers
to sell the empty flats below to the Fezziwig girls!
So come New Year, all three were moving in!
Hurrah! Hurrah! What did Mrs Scrooge think of *that*!
(And would she babysit?)
                              Bob came grinning from the kitchen
with a tray of glasses of Buck's Fizz!
Mrs Fezziwig and Mrs Scrooge
                              cuddled and wept with joy!
And that delightful boy, Tiny Tim, called out,
*"Here you are, Grandma, the sweet that Grandad gave you
every Christmas that he lived! A . . ."*
                              "HUMBUG!"
exclaimed Mrs Scrooge!
"God Bless Us, Every One!" cried Tiny Tim.